First Field Trips

Art Museum

by Cari Meister

Bullfrog
Books

Ideas for Parents and Teachers

Bullfrog Books let children practice reading informational text at the earliest reading levels. Repetition, familiar words, and photo labels support early readers.

Before Reading
- Discuss the cover photo. What does it tell them?
- Look at the picture glossary together. Read and discuss the words.

Read the Book
- "Walk" through the book and look at the photos. Let the child ask questions. Point out the photo labels.
- Read the book to the child, or have him or her read independently.

After Reading
- Prompt the child to think more. Ask: Have you ever been to an art museum? What kind of art did you like best?

Bullfrog Books are published by Jump!
5357 Penn Avenue South
Minneapolis, MN 55419
www.jumplibrary.com

Library of Congress Cataloging-in-Publication Data

Meister, Cari, author.
  Art museum / by Cari Meister.
    pages cm. — (First field trips)
  Includes index.
  ISBN 978-1-62031-293-3 (hardcover: alk. paper) —
  ISBN 978-1-62496-359-9 (ebook)
  1. Art museums—Juvenile literature.
  2. School field trips—Juvenile literature. I. Title.
  N410.M397 2016
  708—dc23
                                    2015032570

Editor: Jenny Fretland VanVoorst
Series Designer: Ellen Huber
Book Designer: Lindaanne Donohoe
Photo Researcher: Lindaanne Donohoe

Photo Credits: Brian VanVoorst/Heidi Ehalt, 3r; Capture Light/Shutterstock.com, 5; Corbis, 16–17; EQRoy/Shutterstock.com, 22tr; iStock, 4, 19; Jorg Hackemann/Shutterstock.com, 1; Popova Valeriya/Shutterstock.com, 3m, 6–7, 22tl, 22br; S-F/Shutterstock.com, 12–13; Shutterstock, cover, 10, 11, 18, 22bl, 23tl; Stefano Tinti/Shutterstock.com, 8–9; Thinkstock, 3l, 23tr; Tom Gowanlock/Shutterstock.com, 24; Yevgen Belich/Shutterstock.com, 14–15.

Printed in the United States of America at Corporate Graphics in North Mankato, Minnesota.

Table of Contents

All Kinds of Art

Where is the class going?

To the art museum!

Sue meets them.

She is a guide.

She talks about the art.

Some pieces were
made long ago.

7

Some are newer.

In the Japan room, Pi sees a scroll.

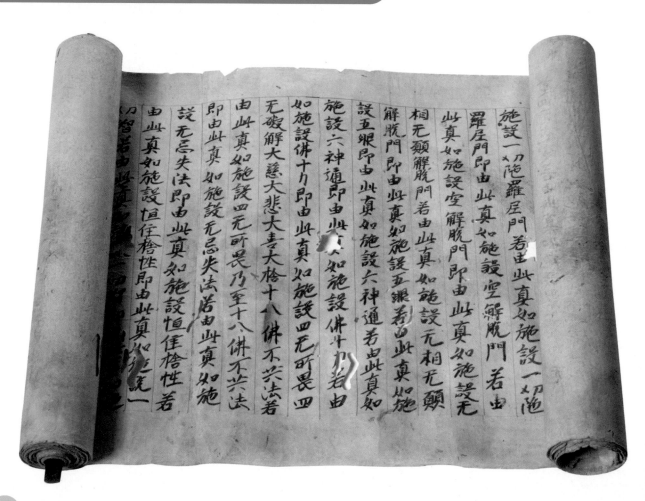

Ann sees a tea set.

Wow!
Look at all the statues.

This one is a warrior.

It is very big.

It is made of marble.

In the painting room,
Al sees a face.

Tia sees a fish.

Dev finds a booth.

It has dress-up things.

He puts on a mask.

What a fun day!

At the Art Museum

painting

sculpture

mask

guide

Picture Glossary

marble
A limestone that takes a high polish and is used in architecture and sculpture.

statue
A likeness (as of a person) sculpted or cast in a solid substance.

scroll
A roll of paper or animal skin on which something is written or engraved.

warrior
A person who is or has been in warfare.

Index

To Learn More

Learning more is as easy as 1, 2, 3.

1) Go to www.factsurfer.com

2) Enter "artmuseum" into the search box.

3) Click the "Surf" button to see a list of websites.

With factsurfer.com, finding more information is just a click away.